The Bloom Effect
A Collection of Poems, Songs, and Haiku's

Airregina Clay

SMART ARTIST PUBLISHING CO.
Do it the smart way.

Copyright © 2018 Airregina Clay

All rights reserved.

ISBN: 978-0-692-10872-7

DEDICATION

I dedicate this book to every girl and the women of color who dare to walk in the authenticity of who they are- YOU ARE WORTHY!

I dedicate this book to every girl and woman around the world who dare to bring their dreams to fruition- WE ARE THE SEEDS OF CHANGE!

Copyright © 2018 by Airregina Clay

All rights reserved. No part of this publication may be reproduced, distributed, or transmitted in any form or by any means, including photocopying, recording, or other electronic or mechanical methods, without the prior written permission of the publisher, except in the case of brief quotations embodied in critical reviews and certain other noncommercial uses permitted by copyright law. For permission requests, write to the publisher, addressed "Attention: Permissions Coordinator," at the address below.

ISBN: 978-0-692-10872-7 (Paperback)

Front cover image by https://pixabay.com.
Book design by Smart Artist Publishing Co.

Printed by Printed by CreateSpace, An Amazon.com Company

First printing edition 2018.

Smart Artist Publishing Co.
www.smartartpub.com
(708) 634-6073

Ordering Information:
Quantity sales: Special discounts are available on quantity purchases by corporations, educational institution, religious organizations, associations, and others. For details, contact the publisher at the information above.

ACKNOWLEDGMENTS

I would like to thank my mother, Yulanda Sykes for your sacrifice, love, strength and unyielding support - you are my inspiration.

To my 4th grade teacher, Ms. Williams who gave me my first poetry writing assignment, you created a space for me to discover my gift.

Thank you to the art form of Hip-Hop for helping to cultivate my dialect, cadence, tone, and delivery of the spoken word.

Thank you to my partner Tova Black for inspiring me to be a better human being.

All honor and glory belong to my lord and savior, Jesus Christ.

Contents

The Bloom Effect 4
Today 7
Lotus Flower Bloom 8
Color 9
No More Waiting 10
Live In The Now 12
Let's Arise 13
Dreams 14
Keep On 15
Work 16
Women Of Yesteryear 17
Break Free 18
Linguistics 19
Fresh Start 20
Save The Children 21
Ugly Truths 22
Reaching For The Light 23
Slipping 24
Conquer 25
Existence 26
Thank You 27
Humanity 29
Conditions 30
Graduation 32
What Will You Do? 33
Purge 35
Color complex 36
Creator 38
I Used To Love U 39
D.A.R.E. 41
Made 2 Win 42

WHY THE LOTUS FLOWER?

I have always had a deep infinity for lotus flowers. As a younger person, I was intrigued by the flowers ability to grow from rivers and muddy places. I had no idea of the lotus history and symbolic meaning.

The lotus flower re-blooms every morning after being covered by mud and water at night. One of the marvelous aspects of this process is that the lotus flower does not show any signs of the murky water or dirt it was once submerged in.

I have grown and learned more about this sacred flower, I have a deeper appreciation for the lesson of rebirth it teaches humanity; we do not have to conform to our environment, but we can rise above it.

The very thing meant to break us, weaken us, and drown us; can be used to grow us- we can be reborn.

THE BLOOM EFFECT

I wanted their respect

They just wanted to see me sweat

I guess to overcome your fears

You must make it through the unrest

Felt like my heart was under water

My mind couldn't catch a breath

I was praying for intervention

Trying to locate my intuition

I dared to be different

Yet, was unsure of my position

Questioned my merit

While mediocrity mirrored in my reflection

Knew I was destined for greatness

So why am I battling with depression?

If pressure makes diamonds

I should shine bright as the sun

If the last shall be first, why haven't I already won?

Didn't realize I was getting back to the basics,

Welcome to "Fundamentals of Life101"

You have to crawl before you walk

Listen before you speak

We were all blind once and couldn't see

I've been on a journey

The road I took led back to me

I woke up and realized I had been in the passenger seat

Driven by inadequacy

While doubt reminded me of the things I couldn't be

Attempting to steal my dreams

I know what's it's like to not hear my own screams!

But somewhere in the midst of all those rocks and hard places

I saw a glimpse of light seep through all of those void spaces

There's more to life than survival

No more walking blind fold

My glass isn't half empty - it's half full

My spirits waking up

I'm so thankful

Cause even when I'm going through

I'm still going

I have a lifetime to learn

I'm still growing
At times my pain shows
But I'm not broken
I pray my transparency heals souls
So the truth of me is glowing

I've been in this process for a while now
Strengthened my broken wings
Now look at this hummingbird sing
My cocoon is starting to open
Shedding those scales of the past
I'm shifting my focus
Aligning my vision
So my consistency matches my conviction
Without struggle there is no progress
This is the Bloom Effect!

TODAY

Joy swept over me

Woke up saying, "I'm alive"

Thankful for newness

LOTUS FLOWER BLOOM

She blooms in sun, heat and rain
She blooms in cold, pain and dirt
Radiantly
Lotus-Flower-Blooms
Exploding with life
Giving beauty by being what she was made to be
Lotus-Flower-Blooms

She expresses more than what you see
She is symbolic of struggle and strength
Laughter and tears
All while overcoming fears
Lotus-Flower-Blooms

She blooms in LA, Chicago, Ohio, and DC
She blooms in Canada, Africa, Haiti, and Beijing
She Blooms with love, genius, talent, and grace
She is born!
She is becoming!
She is learning!
She is achieving!
Lotus-Flower-Blooms

COLOR

Where are we going?

In a world void of color

We live in contrast

NO MORE WAITING

I was waiting for my legs to grow, so I could walk

Waiting for these words to form in my mouth, so I could talk

Waiting on a vision, so I could see

I was waiting to dream

Waiting on permission to be…

That little girl again, with endless hope

Who didn't believe in the word "NO"

Carried the world and its possibilities on her sleeve

Would love freely and let love be!

The power in her!

From Princess, was born to become Queen

So how did I end up waiting?

Didn't realize all this time, I've been delaying

Debating with myself over my own validity

Like God had never spoke to me!

Thought I was in a safe space

Thought I knew my place

Only to realize I didn't recognize those eyes

Didn't recognize that face

Couldn't feel my spirit

Something had changed

Was I really born to make change?

I had been waiting for so long
I forgot the movement of action
There is no passion in passivity
Only condemnation when you take the back seat
Acting like I had the victory, but empty!

I don't have to wait anymore
I'm not running late to make it to my own destiny anymore
I'm going to walk with these legs, though scared
I'm going to speak with this mouth, though hard
I can see with my eyes and my vision is in sight
Although I cry
As long as I live
I will fight!
Cause I don't have the right to hold my light
All this time
The world has been waiting on me.

LIVE IN THE NOW

Yesterday is gone

Today is but a mere breathe

Came, felt, exhaled, gone

LET'S ARISE

My heart bleeds through this pen

For the kids who do not know

That there worth more than silver

Their minds more precious than gold

You just might be that rose from concrete

You have the power to conquer

You were born with a gift

Lion from tribe of Judah

You a prophecy sent

They say pressure makes diamonds

And you been through the fire

Wear your scars with pride

It's your badge you survived

For the wisdom we strive

Off of the knowledge we thrive

It's our time

Let's Arise!

DREAMS

I won't give up

On you anymore; too much

Time has escaped us

KEEP ON

You wake up and don't know how you make it

Don't know if you have the strength to take it

The world is so dim

Where's the light?

It's like you fight to live and live to fight

It's got to be a better way

Cause struggle and your destiny

Someone reached out to me and said- Listen

It ain't over-Hold your head up

You can cry, but don't you lay down

You got to walk now-You got to breathe out

Just breathe now-Breathe now!

And keep on pushing don't give up

Keep on pushing your enough

Keep on pushing when it's rough

Just keep on- Keep on

Keep on pushing you're enough

Keep on pushing when it's tough

Keep on pushing and don't give up

Just Keep on- Keep on

WORK

Breaking old chains takes

The work of hands that refuse

To quit when tired

WOMEN OF YESTERYEAR

It's hard to judge the mind and hearts

Of the women from yesteryear

Though the pain of their decisions

Still linger in the atmosphere

Hanging over us, wrapping us up in secrets and regrets

Life's stresses wore on them like bare feet walking dirt roads

They became one with survival

Going without question

Lived a of life discretion

"Cause my business ain't none of no one else's"

Domestics, Wives, Mothers, Women- but never equal

Gave up so much, only to gain so little

Couldn't complain much, not even a little

Can you blame them for being brittle?

Labeled as the mentally insane

Some checked out, while daughters and sons were violated

Looking for mama to keep them safe

"Child you bet not say that again"

That's yo Daddy, that's yo kin

That's yo uncle, what were you being fast fo?

He didn't mean anything by it

Just deny it

Shhh, be quiet

BREAK FREE

I will never stop

Believing that freedom is

Near for you, break free!

LINGUISTICS

It goes opium melody

Cop 'em poppy happy seeds

Words can get you high

Try a dose

The antidote for free

Mental stimuli be the reason that I melanin-ate

Etymology is the reason that I simulate

This transparent being

Is the ultimate utopia

Serving light beams

Cosmic rays create the culture

I can get you closer to the sun

Than you have ever been

Darkness is the womb

Illumination is the fruit it brings

Let me give you scales and keys

Operatic octave be

 Level of divinity

Third eye, it is the trinity

I am the sacred mystery

Principle of proclivity

Using my witfully

There's never ever ending me

FRESH START

Smile deep from your heart

Laugh away yesterday's pain

Tomorrow is new

SAVE THE CHILDREN

All the kids wake up

Mama still turn't up from last night

So she sleeping

Big brother thinking, How we gone eat?

Ain't had no food since the weekend

Got to go to school though

Can't tell them people

Cause problems, they will start soon

But with the burning in their stomachs

They can't focus

Teacher said they need discipline

But they hungry

They got iPhone and tablets, But they lonely

Screaming out

Please, someone just hold me!

I'm raising myself, I'm only 14

In these cold streets

Who gone save the children?

Who gone save the babies?

They screaming save me!

Can't nobody do but us y'all

Ain't nobody gonna come and do it for us

Can't nobody do but us y'all

Ain't nobody gonna come and do it for us

Ugly Truths

Injustice

Is

IN US

REACHING FOR THE LIGHT

We the chosen

Scholars before college

Never knew I could go further

But I hurdle over obstacles

Never topple -never sink

My future closer in reach

I can taste my dreams like rain on skin

Razor thin is the line between victim and victor

I was born a winner

So I must reconsider my position

I may be greeted with resistance

But I'm standing on solid ground

Even when I fall -I never falter

On my knees I wonder

What's on the hearts of men?

Despite all the war

The sickness and poor

The laws we uphold

The history stole

The darkness is cold

The truth it unfolds

But we keep reaching for the light

We gone be alright

SLIPPING

Optimism can be

Unstable, fleeting like air

I tried to hold you

CONQUER

I hear them talking
Yeah they be watching, but they can't stop me
Yeah they be waiting
They stay debating
They want to know if I'm gone make it
Or will I cave if

All the pressure of the world came falling on my shoulders
Will I sink or swim or will I give up before shore and
Can I stand the pressure when the fires on - the fires on
Will I find my way back home - even if the lights not on?

Conquer, Conquer, Conquer
I'm a
Conquer, Conquer, Conquer

I'm not ever going back to who I used to be
I'm not ever going back, I'm learning to love me
I'm not ever going back to who I used to be
I'm not ever going back, I'm learning to love me
I'm a CONQUER!

EXISTENCE

Do I exist by

Accident, Unexpected

Bi-product of chance?

THANK YOU
(ODE TO GOD)

Don't have the word to express my gratitude

For those many dark days- that you've seen me through

Those many nights that you held me close

Never let me go and whispered in the my ear

Saying "I got something greater planned"

My purpose is in your hands

And when they try to slay you

With the confession of their mouth

My anointing it will surely bring you out

So I'm thankful for…

Your word

Your grace

Your love-It saves

Your truth so pure

I have become

New like a baby born

I have been redeemed

The same power in you

It lives inside of me

I've been awakened
New breaths I'm taking
Cause you have come in
You made everything new
You have come in and made everything new

The moon
The stars
The earth you gave
The sun
Fresh rain
You never change
The same today, tomorrow, forever
I will delight in your pleasure

I've been made new again-I see your halo
You've made me whole again-I see your halo
Have become one again-I see your halo
For that-I thank you, I thank you
I thank you!

HUMANITY

The ability

To except that weakness is

Inevitable

CONDITIONS

Sometimes it's hard to speak

Cause words don't come out right

So I grab my pen and my pad and I write

They ask me, Gina "why you always write sad poetry"?

I say "Life is a killer and don't act like you don't notice that-

Its mass genocide in our communities

Like- babies dying ain't noteworthy to talk about

Another mother cries

And that's why I'm shouting out

That I'm frustrated and contemplating

If collectively, my people would ever rise and see

That God never intended for us to live savage

Ravished by pipe dreams of just being average

Said it's a new day

He selling old weight

He be a King

With peasant schemes

Of buying new gym shoes and fresh jeans

I'm wondering

If this why we suffering?

And the pressure comes from his fellow man

Rather put a gun in his hand

Than teach him how to be a dad

Love his children

Respect his woman

Protect his home

The days are long

We all got to stand up

Women and Man

Yeah we both need to man up

Before times up

And we left stuck

With our hands up

GRADUATION

I wonder if they

Know what is ahead of them?

How soon they grow up

WHAT WILL YOU DO?
(COMMENCEMENT REFLECTIONS)

After the applause and pictures
After the celebrations and dinners
What will you do?
After Facebook post, Tweet updates, and Instagram pics
Forever capturing today's accomplishment
What will you do?

By no means do we minimize this moment
We revel in joy and anticipation
This is the moment we've been waiting for
Praying for and working towards
Studying for and typing till 3:00 in the morning or maybe 4:00
This is the moment we are afforded the luxury to have
That is why we must put a demand on ourselves
Let's spark a deeper examination of critical thought

What will we do with the knowledge that's been taught?
The wisdom received- The lessons and all the readings
With the understanding of the world's transgressions
What will we do with the relationships forged?
The tools and jewels collected along the way
Yes at times we strayed, at times lost faith

But truth always kept us grounded
With God's love and mercy
Grace always abounded
So, what will you do?

Knowing we have an obligation
To care about what we give the world
Through our skill and expertise
Through our merit and good deed
For the bettering of humanity
We've done so much more than received a degree
We've been given a key
And yet, there are still so many doors that need to be open
So what will you do?

With the opportunity to be a conduit of change
Isn't that the Vincentian way?

PURGE

I cried because I

Felt like my power had been

Snatched from my being

COLOR COMPLEX

She asks me: Do you think I'm pretty?
I smile looking into her eyes and say "Yes"
She replies: "Pretty to be a dark skin girl
Or just pretty because I am"?

Being colored is a metaphysical dilemma,
Were still trying to conquer
Wishing I had the simplest of words to make her understand
That her beautiful dark skin glows cause GOD kissed it
Making her a shade different and ambient all its own

Her color is but a reflection of deep melanin from within
Giving life to all things that breathe and sing
She is the SOUL of Beauty
The very concept of full lips, thighs, breast and derriere
Is the hour glass figure!

Her dark skin has been ridiculed and hated
Misunderstood and under represented
Exploited by other brown faces that didn't realize
They were just a different branch growing from the same tree

I told her she was exquisite she was divine
Pyramid glyph would agree that she is Queen
Every range of shade on our color tree
Starts with the original form of BLACK

Showing her current and ancient dynasties of women
That mirrors what she sees everyday
Her very color is the Science
She is the science … Dark skin Sista
With stars in her eyes
Smiling a million moons

Those who are perplexed by your complexion
Don't understand the complexities of
 Being alive and being women and being colored
All at the same, it's quit a fete
So I simply said-
"Your pretty cause you are, but the fact that you have
this dark skin makes it all the more captivating to marvel at".

CREATOR

A writer reflects

Emotions through ideas

Painting every word

I USED TO LOVE U

I used to be in love with you

See you introduced me to a language

I had never spoke, but I felt- in every word

Instantly pulled me into you

Making me feel powerful

It was undefinable

I could only use poetry to capture the moments we shared

A black girl in Hip-hop

Something about the artistry at a young age inspired

Nodding my head to your beats

Rhythmically exposing me to meaning of MC

This was me

You were my voice to melodies

Turning my sonnets into bars

Escaping in your cypher

Amazed that words could create new identities

"You had a strong hold me"

To the point that we would

Walk and talk about everything

But somewhere between-In the midst of bliss

You let other voices come in

You were solid, so why did you lend your ear to them?
They infiltrated your system
Took your story telling, art, and dance
You started tripping hard
Getting angry - hostile
Calling yourself a gangster
Rapping to me about cash, cars, clothes and bling
I was confused
You had been beautiful way
You came with your share of hurt and pain
Frustration over the system -The grit, grime and dirt

But, there was a purpose in your message
And that's what drew me into you
So why would you push me away?
Started infecting my veins with hatred for myself
Glorifying all those things wrong in my community
No, this isn't how this was meant to be!
You used to revere me as Queen
Now bitch and hoe flows out as your lyrics
Who are you?
I used to be in love with you Hip-hop
I used to be in love with you
But, who are you?

D.A.R.E.

(DREAM. AMBITION. RESILIENCE. ENERGY.)

We dare to be the

Difference in a world of

Sameness, we are change

MADE 2 WIN

Feels like I'm opening my eyes for the first time

Like baby being born

Mother seeing child

Seasons- Seasons change

Who knew I was this strong?

I keep on holding on, till day break

I almost made it to the other side

Every peak has valley

I've been to the bottom of ocean

Now I'm coming up for air

I was Made 2 Win

Made 2 win

They could never take what they ain't give

I was Made 2 Win

This is for the dreamer

This is for the seeker

Broken hope and lost purpose

Wondering if it's all worth it

This is for the passion

This is for the chase

You got to take your moment

Never ever wait for what's given

You gotta fight to win

So start living

Today's the gift that you've been given

TODAY'S THE GIFT THAT YOU'VE BEEN GIVEN!

This is victory over issues

Being misused, looked over, and abused

Toast to the power that's within you

We're laughing at what we use to cry about

You have come so far, don't give up now!

You have come so far, you gone make it out!

You have come to far!

You were Made 2 Win

Made 2 Win

They could never take what they ain't give

You were Made 2 Win!

ABOUT THE AUTHOR

Airregina Clay is a Chicago native, born and raised in the city's south side. At a very young age, Airregina had a passion for the arts, people, and social justice.

In 2009 Airregina co-founded The Healing Experience Inc. with her mother Yulanda Sykes. The organization is a non-for-profit dedicated to community and youth resource development in the city of Chicago.

Airregina is the Founder and CEO of Smart Artist Publishing Co., established in 2018.

Airregina has been a writer of poetry for the past 15 years and a spoken word performer for 10 years.

Airregina received her Bachelor of Arts in Public Policy from DePaul University, located in Chicago, Illinois.

www.ingramcontent.com/pod-product-compliance
Lightning Source LLC
Chambersburg PA
CBHW041528090426

42736CB00036B/235